THIS BOOK BELONGS TO

Baby Adriana

from
Uncle Desmond, Travis,
Trevor & Trissette

Our Baby's
First Year

Illustrated by Yvonne Perrin

AWARD PUBLICATIONS LIMITED

MY ARRIVAL

Date _____

Time _____

Place _____

Doctor _____

Nurse _____

MY APPEARANCE

Colour of eyes_____

Colour of hair_____

Complexion_____

Weight_____

Length_____

Circumference of head_____

FIRST PHOTOGRAPH

BIRTH SIGN

BIRTH STONE

FLOWERS RECEIVED

GIFTS

CARDS

COMING HOME

PHOTOGRAPHS

FAMILY TREE

ME

Father

Mother

Grandmother

Grandmother

Grandfather

Grandfather

I WAS NAMED

On the _____ day of _____

At _____

In the Presence of _____

_____

_____

PHOTOGRAPHS

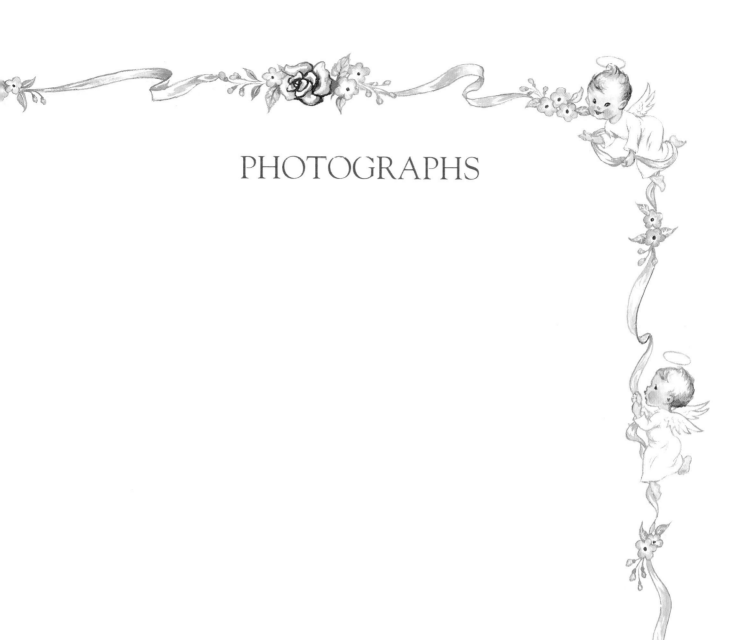

PHOTOGRAPHS

HAND PRINTS

FOOT PRINTS

LOCK OF HAIR

PHOTOGRAPHS

MY PROGRESS

First smile _____

First laugh _____

First rolled over _____

First slept through the night _____

Went into big bath _____

Slept in big cot _____

First ate solid food _____

First tooth _____

First sat up _____

First crawled _____

Stood alone _____

First steps _____

First word _____

RECORD OF MY BABY TEETH

Upper Jaw

Date _____

_____

_____

_____

_____

Date _____

_____

_____

_____

_____

Lower Jaw

IMMUNISATIONS

ILLNESSES

FUNNY THINGS I DID

NAUGHTY THINGS I DID

OUTINGS AND VISITS

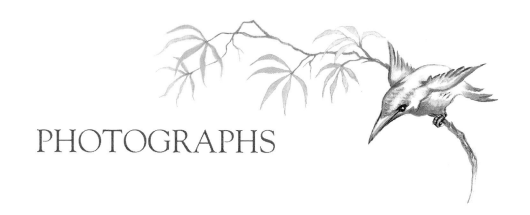

PHOTOGRAPHS

FIRST CHRISTMAS

PHOTOGRAPHS

BEST LOVED BOOKS

MY PETS AND TOYS

FIRST BIRTHDAY

People who came

Presents

RECORD OF GROWTH

My Weight at

1 month _____

2 months _____

3 months _____

4 months _____

5 months _____

6 months _____

7 months _____

8 months _____

9 months _____

10 months _____

11 months _____

12 months _____

My Height at

1 month _____

2 months _____

3 months _____

4 months _____

5 months _____

6 months _____

7 months _____

8 months _____

9 months _____

10 months _____

11 months _____

12 months _____

ISBN 0-86163-712-7

Copyright © 1994 Award Publications Limited

First published 1994
7th impression 2004

Published by Award Publications Limited,
27 Longford Street, London NW1 3DZ

Printed in Singapore